THE LET THEM THEORY
OF MEL ROBBINS

A LIFE-CHANGING TOOL THAT MILLIONS OF PEOPLE CAN'T STOP BELIEVING AND BUYING

RICHARD AUCHTER

FOX WOLFE
PUBLISHERS

CONTENTS

FOREWORD

In December of 2024, author and influencer Mel Robbins released her book *The Let Them Theory: A Life-Changing Tool That Millions of People Can't Stop Talking About.* The book has since sold over 4 million copies in various formats and has been praised across social media as a "life-changing" philosophy. In the increasingly crowded world of pop-psychology and viral self-help books, this one stands out—not for its insight or originality, but for how strikingly empty its premise is. Stripped of its aspirational font and paperback polish, this "life-changing tool" amounts to little more than a motivational slogan stretched far beyond its intellectual limits. The central thesis of the book, repeated ad nauseam, is that you cannot control other people. If someone does something you dislike, the correct response is to simply *let them*. That's it. That's the "theory."

Thus, it quickly becomes clear that the buzz is more about clever marketing than meaningful substance. The single, painfully obvious message that you can't control other people—only your reaction to them-is a truism so well-worn it belongs on the label of a tea bag or at the bottom of an Instagram quote post—not in a book priced as a trans-formational revelation. But wait, it gets worse.

The "theory" essentially encourages readers to respond to frustration, betrayal, disrespect, or any unwanted behavior from others with two words: *let them*. If someone ignores your boundaries? *Let them*. If someone doesn't invite you, doesn't support you, doesn't behave as you hoped? *Let them*. The entire book recycles this phrase like a mantra, wrapped in repetition, anecdote, and hollow empowerment language.

While there's nothing inherently wrong with advocating for acceptance or letting go of control, *The Let Them Theory* adds no novel insight to the conversation. Stoic philosophers, Buddhist monks, and countless self-help authors have long emphasized that we cannot control others—only ourselves. Framing this ancient truth as a groundbreaking discovery feels disingenuous at best, and manipulative at worst.

The writing style is more concerned with virality than depth. It's filled with vague affirmations, self-congratulatory wisdom, and the kind of motivational fluff that gains traction on TikTok because it's easy to digest, not because it's genuinely helpful. The book doesn't offer actionable strategies for people in complex relationships or real psychological frameworks for personal growth. It simply encourages emotional detachment and calls it enlightenment.

Most troubling, perhaps, is how *The Let Them Theory* appears to prey on emotional vulnerability. People experiencing pain or confusion in relationships are promised clarity through this deceptively simple slogan. But rather than guiding them through the nuances of communication, healing, or growth, the book offers a binary, dismissive approach: just *let them*. It demands no effort, no confrontation, no accountability. Just silence. This may feel comforting in the short term, but it's hardly the mark of mature emotional intelligence.

The book functions less as a self-help guide and more as a cleverly packaged cash grab, targeting people desperate for easy answers. Its success hinges on simplicity mistaken for profundity, and on the psychological appeal of non-responsibility. It sells passivity as power, at the cost of real introspection.

In truth, *The Let Them Theory* doesn't need to exist. Its "insight" is something any adult with moderate life experience already knows. The only real revelation here is how effective a catchy phrase and emotionally charged branding can be in monetizing human insecurity.

If you're looking for meaningful growth, you're better off with

Marcus Aurelius, Viktor Frankl, Jordan Peterson, or even your grandmother's advice. At least then, you're not being charged for common sense dressed up as revolutionary wisdom.

Fortunately, the book you are now reading points out the lies and foolishness of *Let Them*, as well as the predatory practices of self-help industry influencers and gurus in general. With this writing, we attempt to show how to recognize and avoid these snake oil sales tactics and the shallow, selfish liars that peddle them. Real growth and healing are possible. However, they look nothing like what *Let Them* and others are selling.

CHAPTER 1

THE RISE OF THE HASHTAG PHILOSOPHY

AT A GLANCE, *THE LET THEM THEORY* LOOKS LIKE EVERY other modern self-help phenomenon: minimalistic cover design, a catchphrase-as-title, and a viral origin story traced not to peer-reviewed research or decades of lived experience, but to a single Instagram post or a clipped, soothing TikTok monologue. In today's cultural climate, that's all it takes. Something vague but comforting catches fire, and suddenly, a slogan becomes a belief system.

The book is less a standalone work of insight and more the natural culmination of a trend we've been watching evolve for over a decade: the hashtag philosophy. These are ideas that aren't built to be thought about—they're built to be shared. Clipped, simplified, decontextual-ized, and memefied until all that remains is emotional candy: sweet, quick, and ultimately unsatisfying.

And *The Let Them Theory* is a textbook case study in how these hollow mantras metastasize into bestsellers.

FROM MEME TO MOVEMENT

The viral spread of "let them" as a personal mantra has less to do with insight and more to do with exhaustion. In an era of fractured attention, relational burnout, and constant digital overstimulation, a phrase like "let them" feels like a balm. It promises release, detachment, peace. It absolves us of the mental labor of confrontation. It offers an easy way out.

You can almost imagine the slow zoom of the camera, the hushed, emotionally neutral voiceover: *"If they don't text back... let them. If they don't see your worth... let them."* The music swells gently. The screen fades to black. You feel seen, perhaps for the first time that day.

But feeling "seen" is not the same as being transformed, and this is where the modern self-help landscape blurs into emotional performance art. *The Let Them Theory* trades in emotional resonance, not practical wisdom. It exploits the momentary relief of being validated, but it offers nothing of depth to support actual healing.

THE NEW SELF-HELP: VIRALITY FIRST, SUBSTANCE LATER

Historically, self-help literature sought to challenge its readers. Dale Carnegie expected you to practice people skills. Stephen Covey asked you to examine your priorities. Viktor Frankl asked you to reckon with suffering. These authors presumed that their readers could handle discomfort and grow through it. They treated you as someone capable of wrestling with real ideas.

In contrast, books like *The Let Them Theory* emerge from a different paradigm altogether. They're written in the grammar of algorithms—short sentences, repeatable slogans, no hard edges. The entire book feels like it was designed to be underlined, highlighted, and posted on Instagram stories. It's not about conveying truth; it's about broadcasting vibes.

This new breed of self-help doesn't aim to teach—it aims to be *liked, shared,* and *purchased en masse.* It is part of the influencer economy. Its success is not measured by how deeply it reshapes someone's life, but by how many people say "OMG I needed this" in the comments.

THE "EMOTIONAL FAST FOOD" ERA

To be clear, the problem isn't that *The Let Them Theory* is short, digestible, or accessible. There's no moral virtue in complexity for complexity's sake. The issue is that the book substitutes simplicity for completeness. It offers spiritual fast food: emotionally satisfying in the moment, but ultimately devoid of the nutrients you need to change your life.

Much like how fast food tricks your brain into thinking it's full by overloading you with salt and sugar, *The Let Them Theory* floods you with validation and gentle detachment to simulate the feeling of enlightenment. But that feeling fades quickly, and the problems it pretends to solve are still waiting for you when the buzz wears off.

This is the emotional equivalent of empty calories—quick dopamine hits at the expense of psychological depth.

WHY IT WORKS ANYWAY

Still, it would be a mistake to underestimate this book's success. What it lacks in substance, it makes up for in cultural timing. We are living through an era of collective fatigue: emotionally, socially, even politically. People are overwhelmed, overextended, and often undersupported. In this exhausted state, the promise of radical simplicity feels like salvation.

The genius of the "let them" mantra is that it tells people exactly what they want to hear: that it's okay to give up, that disengaging is a form of strength, and that you're already doing enough just by walking away. It tells you that you don't need to change, or grow, or struggle with the hard parts of being in relationship with others. You just need to stop caring.

This is profoundly seductive. It's also profoundly incomplete.

WHEN MARKETING MASQUERADES AS WISDOM

The rise of books like *The Let Them Theory* reveals a broader trend: the collapse of the boundary between wellness and marketing. We no longer distinguish between advice and branding. The person who tells you to "let them" isn't your therapist or teacher—they're your favorite lifestyle influencer, building a brand off your clicks, likes, and pain points.

There's nothing inherently wrong with someone profiting from helping others. But when that "help" comes in the form of tautological slogans and reheated common sense, we have to ask: who benefits from this? The answer is simple. The creators do. Not necessarily the readers.

In this context, "let them" functions less like advice and more like a product—prepackaged, branded, and scalable. And it sells precisely because it costs the reader nothing in effort. No risk. No challenge. No emotional labor. Just two words and the illusion of transformation.

Conclusion: Welcome to the Age of Catchphrase Spirituality

The Let Them Theory didn't become a bestseller because it's wise. It became a bestseller because it's frictionless. It asks nothing of you but your agreement. And in a world tired of thinking, reflecting, or struggling, that's a winning formula.

This is the age of hashtag philosophy—where complexity is the enemy, discomfort is taboo, and healing is sold in soundbites.

But real wisdom isn't easy. And the real work of growth doesn't come from a mantra. It comes from wrestling with the messy, uncomfortable, inconvenient parts of being human.

And that, unfortunately, does not sell nearly as well.

CHAPTER 2

A THEORY THAT ISN'T ONE

IF YOU SET ASIDE THE VIRAL PACKAGING, THE SOFT-TONED influencer reels, and the cult-like enthusiasm surrounding *The Let Them Theory*, what remains is a remarkably thin idea, dressed up as doctrine. The book claims to deliver a "life-changing tool" and a "theory" for personal liberation. But what is that theory, exactly?

It can be summarized in four words: *you can't control people.*

To which any emotionally functional adult might reply: *Yes, we know.*

This isn't a theory. It's a basic premise of life. It is as uncontroversial as saying "fire burns" or "rain is wet." Yet *The Let Them Theory* builds an entire book, a brand, and a movement around this commonsense truth, inflating it into a "transformational concept." By doing so, it exposes the hollowness at the heart of much modern self-help: take something obvious, package it as profound, and sell it to people desperate to feel empowered.

Let's be clear—what this book calls a *theory* is not a theory by any meaningful definition of the word.

WHAT A REAL THEORY LOOKS LIKE

Theories, in the philosophical or psychological sense, are meant to explain, predict, or deepen understanding. They are the result of thought, research, testing, or accumulated wisdom. Attachment theory, cognitive dissonance theory, Maslow's hierarchy of needs—these are frameworks that help people comprehend complex behaviors and apply that understanding to their own lives.

Even in the more casual world of self-help, useful "theories" often identify patterns and propose actionable methods. Think of Carol Dweck's *growth mindset*, Stephen Covey's *circle of influence*, or Byron Katie's *The Work*. These are simplifications, yes—but they offer something to work with. They invite reflection and challenge you to test them in your own experience.

The Let Them Theory offers none of this. It does not explore behavior, nor offer tools. It proposes nothing about human psychology except the elementary observation that people are autonomous beings who often do what they want. This is not a theory. It is a fact.

The book is not the codification of insight—it is the commodification of banality.

REBRANDING THE OBVIOUS

Perhaps the cleverest part of *The Let Them Theory* is its ability to convince readers that it's giving them something new. In truth, it simply wraps the most fundamental principle of all interpersonal wisdom—*you cannot control others*—in soft aesthetics and gentle detachment. It strips that truth of its surrounding complexity, rebrands it as a personal superpower, and sells it back to the audience for $20.

This is not insight. This is *intellectual repackaging*, and it is everywhere.

We have entered an era where wisdom is no longer earned—it's curated. Where the bar for being called an "expert" has collapsed under the weight of algorithms, and where the echo chamber of social media has made it possible to mistake repetition for truth. Say something often enough, with enough polish, and someone will call you a visionary.

In this context, *The Let Them Theory* feels less like a philosophical insight and more like a content strategy.

The Lure of Absolutism

Another reason the book's "theory" resonates—despite its thinness—is its absolutism. It offers a blanket response to every interpersonal slight: *let them*. This is intoxicating in its simplicity. But it's also lazy.

Let them ghost you. Let them cross your boundaries. Let them fail you, insult you, ignore you, reject you.

While there's wisdom in choosing peace over conflict, the wholesale application of "let them" as a rule for all human interaction eliminates discernment. It teaches readers to flatten every situation into a binary choice: engage and be harmed or detach and be wise. There is no room for nuance. No consideration of context, of history, of emotional entanglement or power dynamics. Just *let them*—as though that is always the healthiest option.

But life doesn't work that way. Sometimes letting someone go is the right choice. Sometimes confronting someone, or setting a clear boundary, or working through discomfort is the better path. *The Let Them Theory* doesn't help people make these distinctions. It just tells them to retreat and calls that growth.

This isn't wisdom. Its evasion wrapped in a bow.

A Cop-Out Disguised as Clarity

There is something deeply irresponsible about encouraging people to treat all relationship difficulty as a sign to disengage. *The Let Them Theory* promotes a kind of spiritual minimalism that conveniently avoids the hard work of real relational maturity: communication, accountability, forgiveness, and repair.

By branding detachment as enlightenment, the book gives readers permission to never do the difficult work of relating to others in a meaningful way. It doesn't just absolve them from trying—it practically shames them for wanting to. Why waste energy trying to understand someone else's motives or behavior? Just *let them*.

This pseudo-wisdom may feel like clarity, but it's a form of intellectual and emotional laziness. It avoids the hard questions and substitutes certainty for curiosity.

The result? Readers may feel empowered in the moment—but ultimately, they're being encouraged to shrink their emotional world, not expand it.

THE PERFORMANCE OF EMPOWERMENT

One of the more troubling aspects of *The Let Them Theory* is how it equates disengagement with power. In this worldview, walking away is always strong, while engagement is always weak. Silence is strength; confrontation is drama. Distance becomes proof of maturity.

But real empowerment is not about walking away from every difficult situation. Real power is discernment. It's knowing when to lean in and when to step back. It's the courage to have the hard conversation, not just the confidence to avoid it. It's about boundaries, yes—but also about connection, accountability, and repair.

By reducing power to disengagement, *The Let Them Theory* simplifies the human experience into a one-size-fits-all posture of retreat. That's not growth. That's performance.

And for many, it will ultimately be self-defeating.

CONCLUSION: WHEN A SLOGAN PRETENDS TO BE A PHILOSOPHY

The Let Them Theory fails not just because it oversimplifies—but because it pretends not to. It pretends to offer profound clarity when all it gives is self-justifying withdrawal. It calls a truism a theory, a reflex a revolution, a catchphrase a cure.

In reality, it's a hollow slogan with a business model.

This isn't to say the book has no value at all. Sometimes, people need permission to release what they can't control. Sometimes, detachment is a necessary first step toward healing. But when that concept is elevated to an all-encompassing worldview and sold as a philosophy, it becomes dangerous.

It tells people they've arrived when they've barely begun.

CHAPTER 3

THE PSYCHOLOGY OF THE SIMPLISTIC

THERE'S A REASON WHY *THE LET THEM THEORY* RESONATES so strongly with so many people. On its surface, the book's message is comforting. It's short, digestible, and repeatable. But beneath its popularity lies something more revealing: a deep and growing hunger for simplicity in an emotionally overloaded world.

We live in an age of informational overwhelm, emotional exhaustion, and constant uncertainty. Life feels increasingly complex—our relationships, our responsibilities, our self-conceptions. The sheer volume of decisions, anxieties, expectations, and digital interactions has created a culture of cognitive fatigue. In such a climate, the appeal of radical simplicity is more than understandable—it's almost inevitable.

And that's where *The Let Them Theory* enters the picture.

Its success is not an accident of marketing alone. It is rooted in human psychology. It works—at least temporarily—because it speaks to the mind's most basic desires: relief from complexity, resolution without confrontation, and peace without effort. This chapter explores why.

COGNITIVE EASE AND THE NEED FOR SIMPLICITY

In psychology, *cognitive ease* refers to the tendency of the brain to favor information that is simple, clear, and easy to process. Our brains are energy-conserving machines. When confronted with ambiguity, contradiction, or complexity, we instinctively seek shortcuts—mental heuristics that reduce emotional and cognitive strain.

The Let Them Theory functions precisely as one of these shortcuts. It doesn't ask you to analyze, interpret, or confront anything. It simply gives you a rule—"let them"—and invites you to apply it universally. No decision tree. No introspection. Just a two-word formula for everything from being ghosted to being betrayed.

This is not inherently bad. Humans need heuristics to navigate daily life. But the danger comes when these simplifications replace deeper reasoning—when slogans begin to stand in for discernment. That's when mental shortcuts become mental traps.

And that's exactly what *The Let Them Theory* offers: not a tool for clarity, but a trap that masquerades as one.

THE COMFORT OF EMOTIONAL ABSOLUTISM

Another psychological dynamic at play is the comfort of emotional absolutism. When life feels chaotic, emotionally taxing, or uncertain, the mind craves clear answers. Binary thinking—right vs. wrong, good vs. bad, stay vs. go—feels safe. It relieves the brain from having to sit with gray areas, moral complexity, or the discomfort of unresolved feelings.

The Let Them Theory speaks directly to this desire. It offers a blunt solution to every form of interpersonal discomfort: just *let them*. Someone betrays your trust? Let them. Someone doesn't prioritize you? Let them. Someone doesn't meet your emotional needs? Let them.

The theory doesn't encourage nuance. It doesn't ask, *Why does this pattern hurt me? Is there something unresolved in me I need to confront? Could this be repaired or clarified?* It just says *walk away*—and assures you that walking away is always a sign of strength.

This rigid absolutism feels emotionally empowering, but it is ultimately intellectually disempowering. It trains people to avoid depth, to see all conflict as toxic, and to interpret detachment as maturity—when in many cases, it is simply fear in disguise.

THE ILLUSION OF CONTROL THROUGH DISENGAGEMENT

Ironically, though the book is built around the idea of releasing control, what it actually offers is an *illusion of control*—the idea that by choosing disengagement, you've taken back your power. This is a psychological sleight of hand.

Yes, you may not be able to control others, but *letting them* isn't a form of growth if it's just a way of controlling how much reality you have to face. If your "peace" depends on never confronting anyone, never setting a boundary, and never allowing yourself to be challenged, then you're not in control—you're hiding.

But the brain doesn't necessarily register this avoidance as weakness. In fact, it interprets it as agency. You made a decision. You walked away. You chose silence. And in the short term, that decision feels powerful. But in the long term, when relational dysfunctions repeat, when loneliness sets in, when emotional patterns go unexamined, that agency begins to feel hollow.

Disengagement is only strength when it's done from a place of clarity, not fear. *The Let Them Theory* doesn't make that distinction, and because of that, it encourages people to mistake emotional retreat for psychological sovereignty.

EMOTIONAL FAST FOOD: WHY THE BRAIN LOVES SLOGANS

The viral appeal of *The Let Them Theory* is no accident. Slogans stick because they are *cognitively sticky*. The brain loves symmetry, repetition, and rhythm. The phrase "let them" hits all the right notes: it's short, punchy, easy to remember, and feels like closure.

This is the same psychological principle that powers advertising jingles and political catchphrases. In emotionally charged states, people are more receptive to messages that promise quick solutions. The simpler the solution, the greater the relief. The greater the relief, the more loyal the audience.

Books like *The Let Them Theory* rely on this. They are less concerned with provoking thought and more invested in producing a feeling, and that feeling—momentary as it may be—is often mistaken for transformation.

This is not self-help. This is emotional marketing.

EMOTIONAL VULNERABILITY AS A MARKET OPPORTUNITY

At the core of this phenomenon is something profoundly unsettling: the exploitation of emotional vulnerability as a business model.

People don't buy books like *The Let Them Theory* when life is working well. They buy it in the aftermath of betrayal, confusion, breakups, toxic workplace dynamics, family estrangement. In those moments, the desire for simplicity isn't just cognitive—it's emotional. People are looking for certainty, permission, and a narrative that justifies their pain.

Books like this offer a soothing framework: *You're not wrong. You're just wise. And if they hurt you, the smartest thing you can do is let them.* This validation feels good, especially in a culture where people often feel unseen and dismissed. But that emotional reassurance can also become a trap.

Because once you start using "let them" as a universal principle, it becomes difficult to distinguish between true peace and suppressed pain. You may feel lighter, yes. But that lightness might come from burying something you needed to confront.

And therein lies the danger: validation without guidance. Relief without growth.

CONCLUSION: SIMPLE ISN'T ALWAYS STUPID, BUT IT CAN BE DANGEROUS

To be clear, there is nothing inherently wrong with simplicity. Some of the most enduring truths are simple. But simplicity must serve complexity—not erase it. A good philosophy should help us navigate the nuances of our emotional lives, not flatten them.

The Let Them Theory does the latter. It reduces all relationship dynamics to a single response, and in doing so, offers comfort at the expense of clarity. It satisfies the brain's craving for simplicity, but it doesn't nourish the heart or challenge the mind.

This is why it succeeds—not because it's true, but because it's easy. And in a culture addicted to ease, that's more than enough to make a book go viral.

But ease is not the same as freedom. And healing that costs nothing is often worth just as much.

CHAPTER 4

THE DAMAGE OF DETACHMENT DISGUISED AS STRENGTH

ONE OF THE MOST SEDUCTIVE PROMISES *THE LET THEM Theory* makes is that detachment is a form of emotional strength. The book promotes the idea that by "letting them" do whatever they wish—ignore you, betray you, exclude you, misunderstand you—you're engaging in a powerful act of self-respect. It frames silence as superior, retreat as dignified, and disengagement as evolved.

But this framing is not only misleading—it is potentially harmful.

Because while detachment can be healthy in some contexts, *detachment as a lifestyle*—as a universal solution to all relational discomfort—is not empowerment. It is avoidance. And when avoidance becomes your default, what looks like strength on the surface often conceals weakness underneath: fear, resentment, unresolved wounds, and emotional stagnation.

This chapter confronts the idea that "letting them" is always wise. It unpacks how emotional withdrawal can masquerade as maturity, and how *The Let Them Theory* turns healthy boundary-setting into a justification for emotional shutdown.

AVOIDANCE ISN'T WISDOM

The core assumption of *The Let Them Theory* is that disengaging from other people's behavior is a sign of growth. If someone does something you don't like, you shouldn't speak up, seek clarity, or express your needs—you should simply *let them*. Don't react. Don't respond. Don't explain. Just disappear into your own emotional sovereignty.

In certain situations, this may be wise. If a pattern is toxic, repetitive, and resistant to change, then disengagement might indeed be the healthiest path. But in many other cases, disengagement is not wisdom—it's avoidance. It's a refusal to deal with the discomfort of real emotional work: communication, confrontation, negotiation, compromise, vulnerability.

In this sense, *The Let Them Theory* offers not liberation but *permission to emotionally withdraw*. And while that withdrawal may feel calming in the short term, it can have long-term consequences for your relationships, your self-understanding, and your capacity for intimacy.

Avoidance is not maturity. It's just quiet dysfunction.

WHEN BOUNDARIES BECOME BARRIERS

One of the most damaging effects of books like *The Let Them Theory* is how they blur the line between boundaries and walls. A boundary, properly understood, is an act of connection—it says, "This is what I need in order to stay in this relationship in a healthy way." A wall, by contrast, says, "I will remove myself from this entirely, and I won't give you a chance to meet me halfway."

The Let Them Theory consistently encourages the latter.

Instead of encouraging readers to articulate their needs, explain their expectations, or work through tension, it insists that the most powerful move is silence. Don't set the boundary—just vanish. Don't try to repair the rupture—just float above it. Don't clarify your values—just cut them off.

This creates a culture of emotional disengagement, where people equate "not explaining themselves" with being strong. But in reality, refusing to express yourself is not a sign of power. Often, it's a sign of fear—fear of vulnerability, fear of rejection, fear of confrontation.

Healthy boundaries require effort. They require self-awareness, communication, and sometimes conflict. *The Let Them Theory* bypasses all of that and pretends that *not caring* is the same as *knowing your worth.*

It's not.

THE MYTH OF EFFORTLESS PEACE

There's a deeper fantasy being sold in *The Let Them Theory*: the idea that you can achieve peace without effort. If you just withdraw from anyone who doesn't immediately align with your values, your life will become calm and harmonious. The idea that you can float above conflict and enter a Zen-like state of unbothered detachment.

But this is not peace—it's dissociation with branding.

Real peace requires integration. It comes not from running from pain but from working through it. It is the byproduct of facing yourself, facing others, and learning how to stay open while protecting your integrity. It is earned, not given.

The idea that peace comes from simply removing yourself from others' behavior is a fantasy, especially in a world where most of our suffering comes not from strangers, but from those we love. You cannot "let them" your way to healing if the root wound is internal. And yet, that is precisely what this book implies: that disengagement is the endgame.

But people who rely on detachment as a default strategy don't end up more peaceful. They end up lonelier, more bitter, and less emotionally resilient.

THE LONG-TERM COST OF CONSTANT DETACHMENT

Let's follow the advice of *The Let Them Theory* to its logical conclusion. If you consistently disengage from people who frustrate, confuse, or disappoint you, you will eventually run out of people. Every human being you interact with will, at some point, let you down.

What happens then?

You begin to shrink your world. You surround yourself only with those who never challenge you. You mistake safety for health. You confuse comfort with maturity. Over time, your relationships become shallow, your self-perception becomes fragile, and your ability to tolerate discomfort atrophies.

Disengagement as a lifestyle is not sustainable. It might protect you from short-term pain, but it also cuts you off from long-term growth.

Intimacy requires risk. Resilience requires exposure. Healing requires tension. None of that is possible when your entire relational strategy is "let them."

WHEN STRENGTH BECOMES A PERFORMANCE

One of the quiet tragedies of the *Let Them* mindset is that it encourages people to perform strength rather than embody it. You're not told to *become* emotionally grounded—you're told to *appear* emotionally unaffected. You're not taught to build inner peace—you're taught to fake it through distance.

This is a form of spiritual bypassing: using a surface-level spiritual or philosophical concept to avoid deeper emotional work. In this case, the phrase "let them" becomes a script—one you recite to protect yourself from the vulnerability of caring.

You don't say, *"I'm hurt."* You say, *"It's okay. Let them."*

You don't say, *"I want to talk."* You say, *"I don't chase anyone."*

You don't say, *"I feel abandoned."* You say, *"It is what it is."*

The pain is still there. You're just masking it with mantras.

And the longer you perform this strength, the harder it becomes to recognize the parts of you that still need to be seen, held, and healed.

CONCLUSION: THE STRENGTH TO STAY

True strength isn't just about knowing when to walk away. It's also about knowing when to stay. When to speak. When to try again. When to soften. When to set boundaries *and* stay connected. When to risk vulnerability in the name of real intimacy.

The Let Them Theory doesn't teach this kind of strength. It teaches distance. It sells stoicism without the introspection, independence without the growth, and boundaries without the effort.

What it calls strength is often just silence. What it calls peace is often just avoidance. What it calls freedom is often just fear, dressed in affirmations.

And while that may feel good in the short term, it leaves you emotionally malnourished in the long run.

Because life is not just about letting them. Sometimes, it's about *facing them*—and, more importantly, *facing yourself.*

CHAPTER 5

EVERYTHING IT LEAVES OUT

IF *THE LET THEM THEORY* WERE YOUR ONLY GUIDE TO emotional health, you would come away with the impression that the highest form of self-respect is silence, that maturity is synonymous with disengagement, and that the only response to any form of emotional friction is withdrawal.

But real emotional health is far more complex—and far more courageous.

To understand just how thin *The Let Them Theory* is, it's not enough to critique what it says. We must also examine what it doesn't say. Because what's missing from the book isn't trivial—it's essential. In its obsessive repetition of a two-word mantra, the book leaves out the most important aspects of human growth, healing, and connection.

This chapter is about those silences. The absences that reveal the book's true shallowness. The things it *should* include—but doesn't.

1. IT LEAVES OUT ACCOUNTABILITY

There is no serious discussion in *The Let Them Theory* of how we might be contributing to the very dynamics we're encouraged to walk away from. The book speaks as if our only role in relationships is to witness other people's failures, never our own. It assumes our pain is always someone else's fault, and that the only mature response is detachment.

But any honest path to growth requires the question: *What's my part in this?*

- Have I failed to express a need clearly?
- Have I allowed patterns to continue because I was afraid of conflict?
- Have I repeated the same relationship dynamics without addressing the root cause?

The book never invites readers to explore these uncomfortable truths. It offers a convenient binary: if someone isn't what you need, just let them go. No need to examine your own behaviors, expectations, or blind spots.

This omission turns the book from a tool of growth into a shield against introspection. It allows readers to feel superior while remaining unchanged.

2. IT LEAVES OUT COMMUNICATION

One of the most glaring omissions in *The Let Them Theory* is any discussion of communication. There is no exploration of how to express needs, how to repair after conflict, how to listen with empathy, or how to have difficult conversations.

Instead, the book positions all communication as unnecessary or even weak. Why talk it out when you can just "let them"? Why explain your boundaries when you can silently retreat?

But silence isn't always strength. In many cases, silence is the easiest way to ensure nothing changes. Real healing often requires words: awkward, imperfect, emotionally vulnerable words. It requires clarity, confrontation, and sometimes an apology.

By avoiding communication entirely, the book disables the reader's capacity to repair relationships. It tells you that you owe no one anything, but that includes the opportunity for mutual understanding, growth, or closure.

And that isn't strength. That's sabotage, of connection, of account-ability, and trust.

3. IT LEAVES OUT EMOTIONAL NUANCE

The emotional world is not black and white, yet *The Let Them Theory* insists it is. It treats all disappointments the same, all slights as deal-breakers, and all failure to meet expectations as justification for total disengagement.

But people are complicated.

Sometimes people hurt us because they're hurting. Sometimes they disappoint us because they're overwhelmed, confused, or operating from their own wounds. Sometimes people love us deeply, and still fail us in moments.

Maturity requires being able to hold multiple truths at once:

- *They hurt me, and I still care about them.*
- *They were wrong, but they didn't mean to be.*
- *I'm angry, and I'm still willing to talk.*

These are the kinds of emotional tensions that *The Let Them Theory* simply ignores. It doesn't help readers navigate them—it denies they even exist.

And that's dangerous. Because the inability to tolerate emotional complexity leads to shallow relationships and brittle identities. The kind of peace the book offers is one that only exists in emotional isolation.

4. IT LEAVES OUT REPAIR AND RECONNECTION

Every long-term relationship—romantic, familial, or platonic—requires repair. Misunderstandings happen. Conflict is inevitable. Pain is part of the deal. What matters is not whether conflict arises, but whether people have the tools and willingness to work through it.

But *The Let Them Theory* acts as if repair is a waste of energy. As if any disruption is a sign to detach. As if every misstep is a red flag.

There's no space in this worldview for reconciliation. No room for "I was wrong." No hope for "Can we try again?"

By cutting off the possibility of repair, the book turns relationships into disposable transactions. It teaches readers to value self-preservation over connection, self-image over intimacy.

But there is no true intimacy without the willingness to repair. There is no deep love without the capacity to forgive.

And there is no mature self-help philosophy that doesn't acknowledge that.

5. It Leaves Out Empathy

Perhaps the most spiritually bankrupt omission in *The Let Them Theory* is its complete disregard for empathy. Nowhere does it ask readers to consider what someone else might be going through, to understand rather than judge, to inquire rather than assume.

Instead, it encourages readers to see others as either supportive or expendable. You are either aligned with my energy, or you are out. You either meet my needs effortlessly, or I detach. There is no gray area. No room for compassion.

But empathy is not weakness. It's the foundation of emotional intelligence. It's what allows us to be in relationship with imperfect people, which—newsflash—is everyone. A self-help philosophy that teaches you to prioritize your peace at the expense of understanding others is not helping you. It's isolating you.

True peace includes empathy. Real maturity knows how to protect your own space without dehumanizing others.

6. It Leaves Out Self-Examination

Finally, *The Let Them Theory* fails to turn the mirror around. It never asks: *Why do these patterns keep happening to you? Why do these types of people keep showing up in your life? Why are you triggered by this particular dynamic?*

Instead of helping readers understand their own relational patterns, the book reinforces a victim narrative: *They failed you. They disrespected you. They excluded you.* And the answer, every time, is: *Let them.*

But often, what hurts us the most is not just what others do—it's what it brings up inside of us.

A real self-help book would guide the reader inward. It would ask:

- What are the origins of your triggers?
- What wounds are still unhealed?
- What stories are you telling yourself about love, worth, or rejection?

The Let Them Theory skips all of that. It lets readers off the hook. And in doing so, it prevents the very thing it promises to deliver: growth.

CONCLUSION: WHAT'S MISSING SPEAKS LOUDEST

Sometimes, the most revealing thing about a message is what it refuses to say.

The Let Them Theory presents itself as a guide to freedom, strength, and peace. But it never talks about the things that actually lead to those outcomes: accountability, communication, empathy, nuance, repair, and self-examination.

Instead, it offers a shortcut. An emotional escape hatch. A slogan in place of a skill set.

But peace without introspection is just avoidance. Strength without communication is just distance. Boundaries without empathy are just walls.

And any book that leaves out these truths is not helping you grow. It's helping you cope, but poorly.

Because in the end, the parts of ourselves that *we* refuse to face can't be "let them'd" away. They will follow us into every relationship, every disappointment, every silence we choose instead of speaking.

And eventually, if we're honest, we'll realize that it wasn't *them* we needed to let go of.

It was the illusion that healing can happen without looking in the mirror.

CHAPTER 6

THE MONETIZATION OF COMMON SENSE

THERE'S A MOMENT WHEN YOU FIRST READ *THE LET THEM Theory*—if you've read enough psychology, philosophy, or even just lived a little—when you think: *Wait, that's it? That's the whole thing?*

The book's message, boiled down, is simply: you cannot control others, only your reaction to them. This is not a theory. It is not new. It is not revolutionary. It is barely content. It's a phrase you might find stitched on a throw pillow or painted on a reclaimed wood sign in a suburban gift shop.

And yet, *The Let Them Theory* is a bestseller. It is called "life-changing." It has spawned merch, podcast episodes, paid courses, and likely a dozen influencers mimicking the cadence and aesthetic of its delivery.

What does that tell us?

It tells us this: **in today's marketplace of ideas, common sense can be sold back to people at a premium, provided it's packaged well enough.**

This chapter explores how *The Let Them Theory* isn't just an idea—it's a business. A product. A brand. And most importantly, a blueprint for how emotional minimalism becomes commercially profitable.

FROM INSIGHT TO INDUSTRY

There's nothing inherently wrong with selling wisdom. Authors deserve to be compensated for the work they put into distilling ideas, sharing experiences, and offering guidance. But there is a difference between conveying wisdom and commodifying it.

The Let Them Theory leans heavily toward the latter. It takes a recycled axiom—"you can't control other people"—and repackages it as a personal breakthrough. The language is not instructional but viral. The concept is not developed but repeated. The tone is less philosophical and more aspirational—a curated aesthetic of calm detachment, often paired with pale color palettes, slow piano music, and script fonts on social media.

This is not an accident. It's a strategy. The book isn't trying to provoke thought. It's trying to become content.

And that distinction matters, because it reveals the central motive of many viral self-help books today: not to help, but to convert emotion into revenue.

MINIMAL EFFORT, MAXIMUM REVENUE

From a business perspective, *The Let Them Theory* is genius. It cost almost nothing to create, and it yields high emotional return. The author didn't need to do extensive research. There are no clinical studies, no citations, no new frameworks, no interviews, no challenging ideas. Just a slogan, repeated with gentle conviction, dressed in soft-spoken emotional clarity.

Because of its simplicity, the message can be easily sliced into reels, tiles, quotes, tweets, and merch. It is tailor-made for digital consumption. In fact, the book itself could be condensed into a single post—and it often is.

But therein lies the issue. When your product is just a slogan, the entire value proposition becomes marketing. The book is not the end—it's the gateway. Behind it lies a cascade of monetizable offerings:

- Branded journals with "Let Them" quotes.

- Video courses about "Emotional Freedom."
- Affiliate links for calm-inducing teas and self-care kits.
- $297 "masterclasses" on setting boundaries.
- Speaking engagements for corporate audiences who want to appear "emotionally intelligent."

The book is merely the launchpad.
And the emotional fragility of the audience is the fuel.

THE EMOTIONAL ECONOMY

Self-help, especially in the influencer age, has become less about transformation and more about monetizing emotional pain. The success of a book like *The Let Them Theory* depends not on its depth, but on its relatability—and its relatability is rooted in your suffering.

It relies on your exhaustion. Your frustration. Your desire to feel powerful after being made to feel small. It offers you a fantasy: that you can reclaim peace by simply opting out. That you don't have to examine your behavior, explain your emotions, or grow. You just have to "let them."

And for a moment, that feels liberating.

But emotional liberation sold in this form is like a payday loan. You get a hit of clarity now, but you're borrowing against the work you'll still need to do later. Because your relationships will not stop being complex. Your patterns will not dissolve overnight. And eventually, you'll discover that "letting them" didn't resolve anything—it just delayed the reckoning.

In this way, *The Let Them Theory* turns your pain into a product. And you're left feeling "seen"—but not necessarily helped.

BRANDING OVER SUBSTANCE

One of the more insidious qualities of this new wave of self-help is the emphasis on brand identity over intellectual rigor. Books like *The Let Them Theory* aren't just content—they are **lifestyle avatars**.

You're not just buying a book—you're buying into a feeling:

- Calm.
- Detached.
- Above the fray.
- "Unbothered."

This feeling is aesthetically reinforced by every part of the product design: the soft tone, the empty space on the pages, the air of minimalist wisdom. The book itself functions like a mood board—an aspirational symbol of the kind of person you'd like to become: someone who doesn't overthink, doesn't overreact, doesn't get pulled into messiness.

But becoming that person requires actual work. The kind that books like this pretend isn't necessary. And because of that, they don't equip you to grow—they equip you to identify with an idealized version of yourself, while continuing to avoid the harder parts of your own evolution.

You're not becoming more peaceful. You're becoming more performative.

And the brand wins either way.

The Ethics of Selling the Obvious

There's also an ethical question lurking beneath the surface of this business model: *Is it right to sell people what they already know?* Is it right to offer a platitude as a revelation, a slogan as a philosophy, and charge for it under the pretense of wisdom?

When someone is vulnerable—fresh off a breakup, reeling from rejection, questioning their self-worth—they are not just reading casually. They are *searching*. They are hungry for tools. For direction. For hope.

To offer them a slogan in that moment—stripped of context, tools, or challenge—is like offering a placebo to someone with a real illness. They may feel better briefly, but they won't heal. They'll just need more content. More slogans. More reels. More courses.

And that is the point. A truly empowered person stops needing the product.

But a person who mistakes slogans for transformation? They'll keep coming back.

CONCLUSION: PAIN IS PROFITABLE—IF YOU KEEP IT UNRESOLVED

The genius of *The Let Them Theory* is also its indictment: it demonstrates how easily truth can be monetized when wrapped in emotional marketing and sold to people desperate for clarity.

It turns a common-sense observation into a multi-platform enterprise. It flatters the reader while giving them nothing of substance. And it succeeds not because it's profound—but because it's profitable.

This is not a book built to help you. It's a book built to sell to you. And when you realize that, you begin to understand what kind of emotional economy we've created:

- One where pain is profitable.
- One where healing is superficial.
- One where empowerment is simulated.

Because if you actually *heal*, you stop needing their content.
And that's the one thing they can't sell you.

CHAPTER 7

THE CULT OF PASSIVITY

IN MANY WAYS, *THE LET THEM THEORY* IS NOT JUST A BOOK —it's a symptom. It is part of a larger ideological shift that has taken root across modern culture, particularly in online spaces: the glorification of withdrawal, the celebration of disengagement, and the framing of passivity as strength.

We now live in a time where being "unbothered" is a personality trait, where cutting people off is a badge of honor, and where the highest form of emotional intelligence is marketed as complete detachment. This is the rise of what might be called **the cult of passivity**—a worldview that celebrates disconnection and avoids discomfort at all costs.

This chapter explores how *The Let Them Theory* reinforces this cult, why it's so seductive, and what it costs us in the long run.

PASSIVITY DISGUISED AS STRENGTH

The central fallacy of *The Let Them Theory* is its repeated message that withdrawal equals empowerment. It frames walking away as the highest form of self-respect, silence as wisdom, and inaction as emotional maturity. But what it truly promotes is a passive stance toward life: do not respond, do not engage, do not explain—just float away.

This brand of passivity is seductive because it allows people to *feel* strong without ever *being* strong. Real strength requires risk: the risk of rejection, vulnerability, being wrong, or failing. Passivity requires nothing. It offers the illusion of power while demanding no courage, no confrontation, and no depth.

In this way, *The Let Them Theory* enables a retreat from life rather than an engagement with it. It encourages emotional anesthesia and calls it healing.

THE RISE OF EMOTIONAL MINIMALISM

We are witnessing a cultural shift toward emotional minimalism—the idea that less feeling, less investment, less connection equals more peace. Social media is flooded with platitudes reinforcing this idea:

- "Protect your peace."
- "No is a complete sentence."
- "You don't owe anyone anything."
- "Go where you're celebrated, not tolerated."
- "Let them."

On their own, these statements contain kernels of truth. But taken together—and interpreted rigidly—they form a worldview that favors total emotional disengagement. They teach people to view vulnerability as weakness, boundaries as barriers, and others' mistakes as unforgivable.

This emotional minimalism encourages people to build fortresses around their inner lives. It mistakes peace for numbness. It promotes disconnection as clarity. And worst of all, it suggests that the most evolved version of you is the one who *feels the least*.

But emotional minimalism is not resilience. It's resignation.

WHY THIS PHILOSOPHY SPREADS

The cult of passivity thrives because it speaks to a legitimate pain: people are tired. They are exhausted by toxic relationships, overstimulation, and emotional labor. They're burnt out from trying to fix others, explain themselves, or hold together one-sided connections.

Into this exhaustion walks *The Let Them Theory*, offering a gospel of non-effort. A soothing voice that says: *You don't have to try anymore. Just let it all go. Stop caring.*

For the emotionally overwhelmed, this feels like freedom.

But it is not true freedom. True freedom is having the capacity to care *without* losing yourself. It's being able to engage deeply without collapsing. It's having the strength to stay open when everything in you wants to shut down.

What *The Let Them Theory* offers is not freedom. It's a kind of emotional numbing—more bearable, perhaps, but ultimately constrictive.

FROM BOUNDARIES TO BRICK WALLS

In healthy psychology, boundaries are flexible, clear, and rooted in self-awareness. They allow you to stay connected while protecting your needs.

But *The Let Them Theory* promotes boundaries that are static and silent. It teaches people to ghost, ignore, and vanish—without explanation or dialogue.

The result is not boundaries. It's brick walls. And brick walls don't just keep others out—they keep *you* in. They isolate you, calcify your pain, and prevent new connections from forming.

In time, this passive approach can lead to emotional stagnation. You don't grow by never being challenged. You don't mature by avoiding every difficult conversation. You don't find intimacy by disengaging from discomfort.

You just stay safe. Alone. Comfortable—but disconnected.

SOCIAL MEDIA: THE TEMPLE OF THE UNBOTHERED

The cult of passivity has found its most fertile ground in social media, where curated identities and aspirational detachment reign supreme. The "unbothered queen" trope—the stoic, minimalist, soft-spoken woman sipping tea while cutting everyone off—is not just a meme. It's an archetype. A performance.

In this landscape, *The Let Them Theory* is the perfect creed. It affirms the influencer image of calm detachment. It gives people away to spiritualize their silence, to aestheticize their avoidance, and to feel superior while remaining entirely passive.

It doesn't challenge your ego. It feeds it. And in the marketplace of validation, that sells better than truth.

THE LONG-TERM COST OF CHRONIC PASSIVITY

While the cult of passivity may offer temporary relief, it comes at a steep long-term price. Because eventually, life demands more from you. It will not let you remain untouched.

- A partner will need you to stay for the hard conversation.
- A friend will need you to apologize when you're wrong.
- A child will need you to model emotional presence—not distance.
- A grief will ask you to feel more than two sanitized emotions.

When that moment comes, all the "letting them" in the world will not prepare you. Because passivity does not build resilience. It builds a shell.

And shells, by definition, are empty.

WHAT ACTIVE MATURITY LOOKS LIKE

If we want to break free from this cult of emotional disengagement, we must reclaim a vision of growth rooted in action.

Active maturity means:

- Having difficult conversations even when they're uncomfortable.
- Feeling your emotions fully instead of intellectualizing them away.
- Staying connected in the face of conflict.
- Making decisions from clarity, not fear.
- Practicing both compassion and accountability—toward others and yourself.

This is not glamorous. It does not fit neatly into a quote card. It won't get you hundreds of likes on Instagram. But it will build something far more valuable: emotional depth, relational trust, and the capacity to love and be loved without running from it.

CONCLUSION: DON'T JOIN THE CULT—LEAVE IT

The Let Them Theory is not just a book. It is a chapter in a much larger story: a story about a culture that is increasingly afraid of feeling too much, engaging too deeply, or committing to the work of real relationship.

It tells you that the highest wisdom is indifference, that the most evolved people are the ones who don't respond, and that peace lies in passivity.

But you don't need to be unbothered. You need to be *present*. You don't need to "let them." You need to *discern, communicate, and choose.*

Because the point of life is not to be untouchable. It's to be touched —and transformed.

And no mantra, no meme, no bestselling book will ever do that work for you.

CHAPTER 8

WHEN SIMPLICITY BECOMES A LIE

SIMPLICITY IS OFTEN PRAISED AS A VIRTUE—AND RIGHTLY so. In a world saturated with noise, clutter, and complication, there is something beautiful, even powerful, about clarity. Great truths are often simple. So are the most effective solutions. But simplicity becomes dangerous when it is not a bridge to understanding, but a shortcut that bypasses it entirely.

That is the central failure of *The Let Them Theory*: not just that it is simplistic, but that it turns simplicity into a substitute for thought. It doesn't refine the truth—it reduces it. It doesn't make complexity more accessible—it erases complexity altogether.

And when simplicity becomes the only lens through which we're encouraged to view emotional life, what begins as a comforting principle can quietly turn into a lie.

This chapter explores how oversimplification in self-help culture distorts wisdom, misleads readers, and contributes to a larger intellectual erosion in the way we engage with ourselves and others.

The Appeal of the One-Answer World

The Let Them Theory succeeds because it provides a single, elegant solution to a messy, painful reality: when people behave in ways that hurt, disappoint, or confuse you, the answer is simply *let them*. Don't overthink it. Don't explain. Don't analyze. Just step back and release.

This approach is emotionally appealing for the same reason cults of certainty are appealing. In a world filled with ambiguity and unpredictability, people long for answers that *feel* definitive. The less you have to wrestle with something, the more confident you feel in your course of action.

But real life does not offer us one-size-fits-all answers. It is filled with nuance, paradox, contradiction, and context. Simplicity, when applied indiscriminately, becomes a bludgeon. It flattens the world into something unrecognizable.

And it creates a mindset where *questions become threats*—because they might shatter the illusion of clarity.

The Lie of Emotional Uniformity

At the heart of *The Let Them Theory* is the false promise that *all* situations can be handled the same way. It treats every interpersonal challenge as equal, every betrayal as identical, every missed text or broken promise as worthy of the same response: detachment.

But relationships don't exist in a vacuum. A coworker missing a deadline is not the same as a partner cheating on you. A friend forgetting to call back is not the same as a parent manipulating you. Yet the book offers the same prescription in every case: *let them*.

This is where simplicity crosses the line into dishonesty. It tells us that context doesn't matter. That our emotional responses can be standardized. That self-respect means responding the same way to every disappointment.

But emotional growth requires discernment, not uniformity. It means knowing when to speak up and when to stay quiet. When to give grace and when to walk away. When to dig deeper and when to release.

A two-word mantra can't do that for you. It only *pretends* to.

SIMPLICITY AS EMOTIONAL BYPASS

When people are hurting, they often reach for something—*anything*—that makes the pain feel manageable. This is why slogans and affirmations feel so comforting. They give structure to chaos. They create the illusion of control.

But the danger of mantras like "let them" is that they become emotional bypasses—ways to skip the harder, slower, deeper work of healing.

Instead of asking:

- Why did this hurt me so deeply?
- What does this situation reveal about my patterns?
- What is being triggered in me, and why?

You say: *Let them.*

And then you move on—not because the pain is resolved, but because you've convinced yourself that "moving on" is maturity.

In this way, simplicity functions like emotional duct tape. It covers the wound, but it doesn't clean it. And over time, that unhealed wound festers beneath a philosophy of peace.

THE INTELLECTUAL LAZINESS OF OVERSIMPLIFIED ADVICE

There is a troubling trend in modern self-help: the erosion of critical thought. Books like *The Let Them Theory* are part of a genre that favors emotional validation over intellectual challenge. They offer the soothing sound of wisdom without the rigor of actual insight.

This is not a call for elitism or complexity for complexity's sake. Clarity matters. Accessibility matters. But when a book abandons substance in favor of slogans, it is no longer a guide—it is a sedative.

True clarity comes from *engaging* complexity, not avoiding it.

That means asking hard questions. That means offering frameworks, not just affirmations. That means helping readers develop the cognitive and emotional tools to think for themselves, not just repeat what they've been told.

Oversimplified advice may feel empowering, but it ultimately disempowers. It trains people to rely on scripts instead of discernment, reactions instead of reflection, and withdrawal instead of growth.

WHEN SIMPLICITY BECOMES SHAME

One of the subtler consequences of oversimplified self-help is the shame it can produce when the "simple" solution doesn't work.

If *The Let Them Theory* tells you that peace will come as soon as you walk away—and then you walk away and still feel sad, anxious, confused—what conclusion do you draw?

Often, it's that *something must be wrong with you*. Maybe you're not evolved enough. Maybe you're still "attached." Maybe you're doing it wrong.

But the problem is not you. The problem is the lie of the easy fix.

When simplicity is sold as a guaranteed solution, it leaves no room for the complexity of real emotional healing. And when real life fails to conform to the book's promise, the reader blames themselves.

This is not just misleading. It's cruel.

COMPLEXITY IS NOT THE ENEMY—IT'S THE WORK

Real emotional and relational growth requires you to face the messy, contradictory, and inconvenient truths of your own psyche. It asks you to:

- Hold space for people you don't fully understand.
- Sit with feelings that don't resolve quickly.
- Engage with your own patterns and projections.
- Navigate relationships that defy tidy explanations.

That's what makes it *real*.

Simplicity can be a powerful doorway into deeper truths. But it is never the whole truth. And when it's mistaken for the destination, it becomes a dead end.

The work of becoming emotionally whole is not reducible to a catchphrase.

CONCLUSION: DEMAND MORE THAN MANTRAS

If *The Let Them Theory* were just a motivational quote, its simplicity would be harmless. But it presents itself as a worldview. A philosophy. A "life-changing tool."

And that's where it fails.

Because real life-changing tools do not erase complexity. They *equip* you to navigate it. They make you more capable, more aware, more resilient—not just more detached.

The next time a book offers you a simple answer to your most complicated emotions, pause. Ask yourself:

- Is this helping me grow?
- Or is this helping me *avoid* growth?
- Because in the end, there is a world of difference between *simple truths*—and the *lie of simplicity*.

CHAPTER 9

THE MARKET FOR MAGIC WORDS

WE LIVE IN A CULTURE THAT IS INCREASINGLY ALLERGIC TO complexity. The rise of social media, short-form video, and algorithm-driven platforms has reshaped the way we consume ideas. In this world, nuance doesn't trend. Subtlety doesn't scale. What sells is clarity—**or, more accurately, the illusion of it.**

In that context, *The Let Them Theory* is not just a slogan masquerading as wisdom. It's a product of a larger marketplace: the **market for magic words.** These are the catchy phrases, bumper-sticker mantras, and therapeutic buzzwords that promise transformation without the mess.

They're short. They're shareable. They're easy to repeat and even easier to misunderstand. But most importantly—they're *sellable*.

This chapter explores how an entire economy has developed around these magic words, why we're so eager to buy them, and how they're failing to deliver on their promises.

WE'RE NOT LOOKING FOR TOOLS—WE'RE LOOKING FOR SPELLS

When someone is in pain, overwhelmed, or desperate for direction, they're not always looking for a method. They're looking for **a spell**—a phrase that makes the pain stop. Something that feels like control in the face of chaos.

That's what "let them" is. It's not a philosophy. It's a spell.

It says:

- *You don't have to care anymore.*
- *You don't have to feel rejected.*
- *You don't have to explain yourself.*
- *You don't have to do the work.*

It's two words that *sound* like a boundary, *feel* like clarity, and *promise* a kind of closure.

And in a moment of emotional confusion, that spell can feel like salvation. But that's exactly why it sells—because it's not offering work, it's offering relief.

CATCHPHRASES ARE THE NEW SELF-HELP

Self-help has evolved. Once, it meant long-form books, structured programs, or in-depth introspection. Now it means a swipeable quote, a 30-second reel, or a PDF workbook sold via Instagram story.

Instead of frameworks, we now get **phrases-as-products**:

- "Let them."
- "No is a full sentence."
- "Protect your peace."
- "Energy is everything."
- "If it costs you your peace, it's too expensive."

Each of these sounds empowering in isolation. But when used indiscriminately, they become evasive. They give people language for disengagement without discernment. And they're churned out by an industry that understands one thing: **people in pain will pay for relief.**

The Let Them Theory is the logical endpoint of this model. It's the monetization of a meme. A phrase that could easily be a caption is stretched into an identity. And people buy it—not because it changes their lives, but because it validates the feelings they already have and gives them an easy way out.

How the Economy of Pain Works

In the economy of magic words, pain is the currency—and attention is the transaction.

Here's how the cycle works:

1. You experience emotional distress.
2. You search for clarity or relief online.
3. You're served a short, emotionally resonant piece of content —a quote, a voiceover, a still image with text overlay.
4. It feels true. It feels immediate. It "resonates."
5. You share it.
6. You follow the creator.
7. You buy the book, the journal, the course, or the coaching session behind it.

What was once a moment of internal distress becomes a click, a follow, a purchase. The emotion was real. The solution was commodified. And the pain? That remains just unhealed enough to keep the cycle going.

Because magic words don't solve anything. They soothe. They sedate. They *simulate* clarity without requiring actual work.

The Dangerous Flexibility of Magic Words

One of the most problematic features of these phrases is their **context-free flexibility.** "Let them," for example, can mean:

- Walk away from an abusive partner.
- Ignore your emotionally avoidant friend.
- Accept that your coworker doesn't like you.
- Stop explaining yourself to your family.

Each of these situations is radically different. Each requires a different psychological response. But the same phrase—"let them"—is offered for all. This is not helpful. It's harmful.

It teaches people to **flatten their emotional landscape**, to see all disappointment through the same lens of release. It conditions you to believe that withdrawal is always the right move, and that engagement is always weakness.

But healing doesn't come from repeating vague slogans. It comes from *understanding when, why, and how to act differently*.

Magic words don't teach that. They just give you permission to check out.

INFLUENCE IS MEASURED IN SIMPLICITY, NOT ACCURACY

The new self-help economy is not built to foster depth. It's built to generate scale. And scale requires simplicity.

This is why influencers repeat the same advice daily, in slightly different forms. It's why their videos have the same cadence. Why the captions recycle phrases like:

- "This is your reminder that..."
- "Read that again."
- "You needed to hear this."

It's not that the advice is false. It's that it's *strategically empty*—designed to sound wise while demanding no examination, no context, no application.

The Let Them Theory wins in this environment because it is perfectly engineered for virality. It's short. It's emotional. It doesn't require explanation. And best of all—it sounds like something you already believe.

That's not wisdom. That's emotional marketing.

When Language Becomes a Wall

Language should expand our world, help us articulate our experiences, and connect us to others. But magic words often do the opposite. They reduce our options. They end conversations before they start.

When someone says "let them" in response to a complex issue, they're not engaging—they're *retreating behind language.*

And that retreat is often permanent. Because once you frame emotional disengagement as empowerment, there's little motivation to explore the nuance. Why reflect when you can repeat? Why question when you've already "let them"?

In this way, magic words become **linguistic armor**—used not to heal, but to shield. And over time, that armor becomes a prison.

The Cost of Mass-Produced Insight

There's something tragically ironic about a culture that claims to be obsessed with healing while refusing to sit still long enough to do the work. We keep buying books, watching videos, saving quotes—and still feeling stuck.

Why?

Because magic words don't work when the problem is internal complexity.

They don't help you:

- Process grief.
- Navigate betrayal.
- Face childhood wounds.
- Take accountability.
- Learn to communicate under stress.

They can *hint* at what's possible. They can *inspire* a direction. But without structure, tools, or reflection, they can't deliver on what they promise.

They're mass-produced insight for mass-consumed pain.

CONCLUSION: DON'T SETTLE FOR MAGIC—DO THE WORK

The Let Them Theory belongs to an industry built not on transformation, but on transaction. It offers language in place of tools, detachment in place of discernment, and ease in place of effort.

But no phrase, no matter how viral, can do the hard work of living for you.

Real growth is slow. It is unmarketable. It is rarely aesthetic. It doesn't fit in a carousel post. And it cannot be sold in two words.

So the next time someone offers you a magic word, ask yourself:

- What is this costing me in complexity?
- What conversation am I avoiding?
- What work am I outsourcing to language?

Because healing is not magic. Its movement.
And no phrase, however catchy, will take that step for you.

CHAPTER 10

BUILDING BETTER BULLSHIT DETECTORS

By now, the shape of the problem is clear. *The Let Them Theory* is not a revolutionary insight, nor is it a transformative philosophy. It is the latest entry in a long line of simplistic slogans sold as self-help—emotional fast food packaged as soul-level nutrition. It does not equip you for growth. It sedates you into passivity.

But this chapter is not about the book. It's about *you*.

Specifically, it's about helping you sharpen your ability to tell the difference between a self-help idea that actually helps—and one that just sounds good.

Because the problem is not just *The Let Them Theory*. It's the entire cottage industry of comfort-first, thought-later advice that's being pushed online, in bookstores, and through influencers with coaching funnels and passive income dreams.

It's time to build better **bullshit detectors.** Not to become cynical —but to become discerning. Not to stop seeking growth—but to know where to find it—and when you're being sold a performance instead.

This chapter offers the tools, questions, and mental frameworks you need to protect yourself from oversimplified advice, shallow empowerment, and emotionally exploitative messaging masquerading as wisdom.

THE COST OF UNCRITICAL CONSUMPTION

When we consume emotional advice without filters—especially during times of vulnerability—we risk internalizing messages that:

- Dull our discernment.
- Reinforce false narratives about strength, boundaries, or healing.
- Lead to isolation disguised as empowerment.
- Encourage permanent detachment instead of adaptive growth.

Without critical thinking, even the most well-meaning messages can morph into harmful patterns.

And in a culture where viral ideas are rarely questioned, the ability to think for yourself is not just a skill—it's self-defense.

HOW TO SPOT EMOTIONAL BULLSHIT: KEY INDICATORS

Let's walk through the common red flags of "bullshit" self-help content —ideas that may sound deep, but fail the test of depth, utility, or honesty.

1. It Overgeneralizes Every Situation

If the advice claims to apply to *every* relationship, *every* dynamic, and *every* type of pain—it's likely too vague to be helpful. Real emotional work depends on context.

Example:

"Let them" as the go-to advice for betrayal, rejection, minor misunderstandings, and workplace issues? That's not insight. That's laziness.

2. It Encourages Disengagement Instead of Discernment

If the message always leads to silence, withdrawal, or emotional numbing—rather than evaluation, communication, or reflection—it's promoting avoidance, not empowerment.

Ask: *Is this helping me grow, or just check out?*

3. It Appeals to the Ego Instead of Challenging It

True self-help makes you uncomfortable before it makes you better.

If the advice only affirms that you're always right, always wise, always the victim—it's not growth. It's ego grooming.

Ask: *Does this challenge me to be accountable, or just let me feel superior?*

4. It Prioritizes Aesthetics Over Application

If the idea sounds good on a mug, tote bag, or Instagram quote card but can't be meaningfully applied in real life—proceed with caution.

Ask: *Can I actually use this? Or is it just something to repeat to myself?*

5. It Turns Complexity Into a Catchphrase

If a book reduces human emotion into one-size-fits-all phrases, it's not simplifying—it's flattening. Complexity is not the enemy. It's the material of healing.

Ask: *Is this helping me navigate nuance—or ignore it?*

10 CRITICAL QUESTIONS TO ASK BEFORE YOU ACCEPT ANYSELF-HELP ADVICE

1. What is this idea asking me to do?
2. Is it encouraging engagement or detachment? Reflection or rejection?
3. Is it true across all contexts—or just convenient in this one?
4. Does it help me take responsibility—or just blame others?
5. Does it support connection—or justify withdrawal?
6. Am I using this idea to avoid a hard conversation?
7. Does it reflect the emotional maturity I want to develop—or just the comfort I want right now?
8. Is the idea coming from someone with lived experience—or just someone building a brand?
9. Can I see how this idea would *work* in real life, or only in theory?
10. How does this advice feel after the initial emotional hit wears off?
11. Would I teach this principle to someone I love—or does it only "work" because I'm in pain?

These questions aren't meant to paralyze you. They're meant to wake you up—because wisdom often sounds quiet and complicated. Bullshit sounds like a mic drop.

THE ROLE OF DISCOMFORT IN REAL GROWTH

Here's an uncomfortable truth that most self-help avoids: **growth hurts.**

- It hurts to realize you've been avoiding hard truths.
- It hurts to admit you've played a role in your own suffering.
- It hurts to confront someone you love.
- It hurts to stay present with a wound you'd rather spiritualize away.

But this is *productive* pain—not the kind that keeps you stuck, but the kind that moves you through. If the advice you're consuming never invites discomfort, it's not inviting transformation. It's selling sedation.

And sedation is not healing. It's just silence with good branding.

WHAT REAL EMPOWERMENT LOOKS LIKE

Let's contrast all this with what real self-help—what real *help*—actually looks like:

- It's specific. Not vague or universal.
- It teaches tools, not just ideas.
- It invites personal responsibility *and* compassion.
- It honors complexity without making you feel broken.
- It helps you act, not just emote.

Real empowerment feels quieter than viral advice. It takes longer. It doesn't always sound clever. But it sticks. And over time, it builds something no slogan ever will: *resilience.*

CONCLUSION: BURN THE SCRIPTS—WRITE YOUR OWN

The most powerful thing you can do in a world of repackaged platitudes is **think for yourself**.

Let others chase trends. Let others build brands. Let others buy and sell magic words.

You? Build your bullshit detector. Interrogate easy answers. Choose depth over dopamine. And remember: the truth is rarely viral—but it will change you.

Because in the end, slogans won't save you. Self-awareness might.

CHAPTER 11

WHAT REAL GROWTH LOOKS LIKE

AFTER TEN CHAPTERS DISMANTLING THE HOLLOW PREMISE, emotional oversimplification, and commercial motives behind *The Let Them Theory*, we reach a natural question: **if this isn't what growth looks like, then what is?**

If "letting them" is too often a slogan for disengagement, what does true empowerment require? If emotional distance masquerading as peace leaves us lonely, reactive, or stuck—what's the alternative?

This chapter is not just a rebuttal to what *The Let Them Theory* gets wrong. It is a sketch of what authentic personal growth requires: not two-word mantras, but deep engagement. Not passive detachment, but active participation in our own transformation.

Because real growth is possible. But it demands what the book refuses to offer: discomfort, responsibility, complexity, and courage.

1. Growth Begins With Self-Confrontation

The first step in any honest personal evolution is *facing yourself*. Not the curated version. Not the performance of wisdom. But the flawed, reactive, confused self that you usually keep hidden.

This is the part of growth that no trending self-help reel can replace. It means asking:

- Why do I attract the same patterns in relationships?
- What part of me benefits from staying passive, silent, or avoidant?
- What am I still blaming others for that I've never really tried to work through?

These are not comfortable questions. But comfort is not the goal. Growth *requires* that we go inward, not just "let them" go outward.

In contrast, *The Let Them Theory* allows people to skip this confrontation. It lets you preserve your self-image, sidestep your own baggage, and walk away from difficult dynamics without ever asking why you were drawn to them in the first place.

But until you confront your own role, your own wounds, your own stories—you're not evolving. You're just rearranging your avoidance.

2. Growth Involves Boundaries—But With Compassion

Boundaries are essential for mental health. But healthy boundaries are not a shutdown. They are a bridge: a way to stay connected to others while remaining connected to yourself.

A real boundary sounds like: *"I care about you, and this behavior doesn't work for me."* Or: *"This is what I need in order to stay in this relationship with integrity."*

It invites clarity. It offers dignity to both parties. It *preserves* the relationship where possible, rather than discard it at the first sign of discomfort.

But *The Let Them Theory* skips this step entirely. It reduces boundary-setting to silence. It teaches you that not responding is power. But in reality, refusing to communicate is often just another form of control: you get to protect your peace without doing the work of empathy or repair.

True growth means learning to articulate your needs—not weaponize your absence.

It's not "let them" as a dismissal. It's "let's talk about it"—and being strong enough to stay in that conversation, even when it's hard.

3. Growth Includes Repair, Not Just Removal

Not every relationship can be fixed. Not every wound should be reopened. But real growth requires the ability to *try*. It means learning how to repair ruptures when possible—because without that skill, every connection becomes disposable.

A mature person knows how to:

- Acknowledge their own contribution to a problem.
- Apologize without defensiveness.
- Listen without preparing a rebuttal.
- Stay in the room emotionally, even when it's uncomfortable.

Books like *The Let Them Theory* train you to cut ties. But life rarely gives us the luxury of permanent exits. Family, coworkers, long-term friendships, co-parenting—all of these require repair skills, not just detachment.

True growth means developing the ability to *stay*—to do the messy work of forgiveness, clarification, and mutual change. Not because it's easy, but because it's worth it.

4. Growth Requires Emotional Fluency

Real personal development means building emotional intelligence —the ability to feel, identify, and express your emotions rather than repress or bypass them.

The Let Them Theory offers emotional simplicity, but real life is anything but simple. A single situation can evoke anger, sadness, fear, desire, and shame all at once. Growth means learning how to sit with those layers, not dismiss them with two words.

Emotional fluency involves:

- Naming your feelings with specificity: *I feel disappointed,* not just *mad.*
- Asking what those feelings are trying to teach you.
- Expressing them constructively, rather than suppressing or exploding.

Detachment often avoids this fluency. It's easier to numb, withdraw, or declare yourself "unbothered" than it is to admit, *I'm hurt.* But emotional maturity comes from learning to feel *everything*—not just what's convenient.

And there's nothing mature about pretending you don't care just because it's trendy.

5. Growth Embraces Nuance, Not Certainty

A real philosophy of personal development doesn't hand you a universal answer. It hands you tools—and teaches you how to use them depending on the context.

The Let Them Theory offers a one-size-fits-all response: disengage. Walk away. Don't explain.

But real life requires nuance:

- Sometimes you should walk away. Sometimes you should stay and speak up.
- Sometimes you're being mistreated. Sometimes you're misinterpreting.
- Sometimes silence is power. Sometimes silence is punishment.

Mature people don't apply slogans to every situation. They pause. They reflect. They ask better questions. They seek to understand the difference between self-protection and emotional avoidance.

Growth is not about clinging to a mantra. It's about cultivating the discernment to know when the mantra applies—and when it's a shield.

6. Growth Prioritizes Depth Over Image

One of the deepest problems with the *Let Them* mindset is that it rewards appearances. You appear calm. You appear detached. You appear above it all.

But real growth is rarely pretty. It's awkward. It's messy. It often looks like crying in therapy, stumbling through a hard conversation, or realizing you've been wrong.

Growth is not something you broadcast. It's something you live. It's not a performance for others—it's an inward transformation that changes how you see, speak, and relate.

The moment your personal development becomes a brand, you're no longer growing—you're curating.

And the path back to authenticity begins where the branding ends.

7. Growth Is Action, Not Aesthetic

Ultimately, the most powerful difference between real growth and the faux growth promoted by books like *The Let Them Theory* is this:

Real growth changes how you act—not just how you feel.

It gives you:

- New relational patterns.
- Healthier communication habits.
- Clearer self-awareness.
- Deeper connections.

Not just better-sounding captions or more followers who admire your "peace."

Letting go is a part of growth. But so is leaning in. So is repairing. So is being vulnerable, messy, confused, and still showing up for your life instead of retreating into a curated illusion of strength.

CONCLUSION: DON'T LET THEM FOOL YOU—YOU'RE CAPABLE OF MORE

Books like *The Let Them Theory* sell you a picture of growth that asks nothing of you. That's what makes it seductive. But it's also what makes it hollow.

You don't need to be told that you can't control others. You already know that.

What you need is the courage to examine yourself, the strength to stay connected in the face of pain, and the wisdom to discern when to walk away—and when to do the deeper work of staying.

That's what real growth looks like.

And it will never fit into a slogan.

CHAPTER 12

LET THEM... KEEP SCROLLING

AT THE END OF ALL OF THIS—AFTER PEELING BACK THE SOFT aesthetic, the gentle slogans, the hollow advice, and the viral sheen—what's left of *The Let Them Theory*?

Two words. An emotional shrug. A sellable phrase designed to feel like a revelation.

It's not. It's not even helpful. It's not even necessary.

This final chapter isn't a takedown—it's a release. Because just as *The Let Them Theory* invites us to passively "let" others do whatever they want, we, too, can "let" books like this pass through our culture without granting them the reverence they don't deserve.

Let them post it. Let them praise it. Let them share it. Let them call it profound.

But don't mistake virality for value. And don't confuse resonance with rigor. Because you—if you've read this far—are capable of far more than performative detachment and two-word solutions.

THE PROBLEM ISN'T JUST THE BOOK—IT'S THE APPETITE FOR EASE

The Let Them Theory didn't invent emotional disengagement. It just packaged it nicely.

It gives language to a desire many people already have: the desire to stop trying, stop explaining, stop feeling so much. In a world that constantly demands our energy, attention, and care, this kind of "empowerment-through-withdrawal" feels like a balm.

But at its core, it's just another kind of spiritualized numbness.

The real issue isn't that people want to disengage. It's that they've been taught disengagement is the only form of protection - that walking away is the only path to peace, and that the more detached you are, the more mature you must be.

That's the lie. That's what we have to unlearn.

Because peace is not the absence of effort. Peace is the product of effort that *works.*

YOU DESERVE MORE THAN A MEME

Books like *The Let Them Theory* treat you like a consumer of feelings, not a builder of character. They assume you don't want to do the work. They flatter your pain and then sell it back to you as a lifestyle.

But real growth is for people who are ready to:

- Ask hard questions.
- Take responsibility for their own emotional patterns.
- Heal without performing it.
- Say things like, *I don't know, I was wrong,* or *Let's talk.*
- These aren't popular. They don't trend. They don't sound like empowerment. But they are.

You deserve more than magic words. You deserve *truth.* And truth will never be reduced to two syllables.

A BETTER PATH FORWARD

Instead of "let them," what if your guiding principle was:

- *Understand them.*
- *Express yourself to them.*
- *Challenge them—with kindness.*
- *Decide—consciously—whether they belong in your life.*

This is harder. It's slower. It's not always as immediately satisfying. But it leads somewhere worth going.

Because growth is not a destination. It's a process. A messy, non-linear, often exhausting process of becoming someone who no longer needs to hide behind mantras.

WHAT YOU CAN DO INSTEAD

If you've found yourself drawn to books like *The Let Them Theory*, that doesn't make you gullible. It makes you human. You were looking for peace. You were looking for a way to manage your emotional landscape. That is valid.

But now you know what to do next:

- Trade slogans for frameworks.
- Trade passive disengagement for active discernment.
- Read work that respects your intelligence—not just your insecurities.
- Demand more from your emotional tools.
- Build depth. Build skill. Build courage.

Let others keep chasing comfort. You? You build clarity.

LET THEM... KEEP SCROLLING

Let the influencers sell shortcuts. Let the branding agencies package detachment as dignity. Let the feeds overflow with pseudo-wisdom. Let them think that "letting them" is the end of the story.

But you?

You'll keep thinking. You'll keep asking. You'll keep growing.

You'll build relationships that stretch you. You'll engage with emotions that challenge you. You'll use language that heals instead of hides.

And when someone tries to sell you yet another emotionally soothing soundbite, you'll smell the bullshit and know better.

You are not a slogan. You are not a caption. You are not a passive participant in your own life.

You are a person capable of real reflection, real relationship, and real change.

The world needs more of that. Not more silence. Not more slogans. Not more detachment sold as dignity.

So the next time someone says "let them," ask:

- What would it mean to *understand* them?
- What would it mean to *respond* with maturity?
- What would it mean to *act*, not just *opt out*?

That's where the real transformation lives. Not in the phrase. Not in the brand. But in you.

About the Author

With undergraduate and graduate degrees in religion and history, and post-graduate/doctoral studies in sociology, Richard Auchter is a thinker, scholar, observer, and documenter of the human experience.

Sign up to get updates about his writing at
    www.richardauchter.com

ALSO BY RICHARD AUCHTER

*The Matthew Principle: How The World Really Works - Why Success
Accumulates and Failure Compounds*

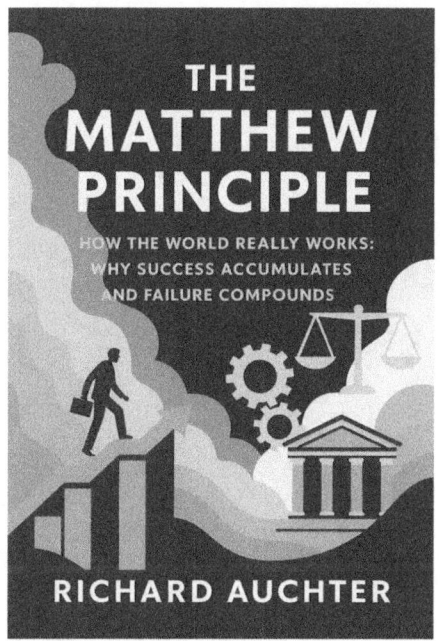

Available at all major booksellers

www.richardauchter.com